The Little Black Book of

Fill-in-the-Blank Wedding Speeches

By

Jerusalem Singleton

The methods described within this book are the author's personal thoughts. They are not intended to be a definitive set of instructions for this project. You may discover there are other methods and materials to accomplish the same end result.

The Little Black Book of Fill-in-the-blank Wedding Speeches

ISBN-13: 978-1481818780

ISBN-10: 1481818783

Editor: Margo McCoy

Author: Jerusalem Singleton

First Edition/ Volume 1: September 2014

To the person who showed me just how wide my wingspan is.

...

Cheers!

CONTENTS

Forward

As a wedding DJ and Master of Ceremonies, I regularly hear members of the bridal party say,

"I don't know what to write," or "I'm so nervous about my speech."

Alternatively, I hear the same jokes and quotes every other week. That's because it's so easy to fall into the "search engine" standard speech trap when getting ideas on writing a wedding speech or toast. Chances are if you found them easily, so did a lot of others.

I too have had writers block every now and then and have called on Jerusalem to write for me.

I like this book because it's easy to read and doesn't go on and on. Jerusalem has a great writing style and sticks to what's important. In this book you will quickly learn what is needed to put together a great speech or toast. While it's called "Fill in the blank wedding speeches," Jerusalem provides you with the guidelines and, through adding your own unique stories, make it personal, bringing an added joy and warmth to your reception.

Remember, you don't have to write a master piece; it can be kept short and sweet. It's better leaving people wanting more than wishing you would shut up, and this book helps you achieve that!

Wedding DJ Specialist (Australia)

Preface

I know that you're having a hard time and have been hoping for a solution ever since you were asked to write a speech for a wedding. Today, you've just picked up the answer to your prayers. As soon as your prayer went up, the Powers that Be sent me a note explaining your situation. Yes. I am your answer … and I am here to serve you! You hold in your hands the quickest, easiest and the most fun way to write your wedding speech …

The Little Black Book of <u>Fill-in-the-Blank</u> Wedding Speeches.

So, you've been asked to do a toast at a wedding - one of the most important days in someone's life. Your heart starts pumping. You feel the sweat forming on your brow. It's a big responsibility to speak in front of a large group of people who will be hanging on to your every word and expecting you to say something sweet, funny or profound. In the beginning, you think to yourself,

"What an honor it is to be asked to be the best man or maid of honor."

Or,

"What an honor it is to be asked to say a few words at the wedding."

But secretly, I know what you're really thinking.

"How am I going to do this?"

"What do I say?"

Sound familiar? Well my friend, it's time you settle down and take a deep breath, (In fact, I actually have a section about deep breathing right here in this book). This book was written just for you. It's a quick and easy guide to writing a wedding speech with YOU in mind! All you have to do is just add YOUR memories, YOUR experiences and YOUR personality and after just a few minutes (like 5-10 … no, seriously), presto! You're well on your way to giving a spectacular wedding speech that will wow the bride, the groom and the entire audience. And you'll have fun doing it too. It's as simple as filling in the blanks!

READY? SET? GO!

INTRODUCTION:

As the youngest child of seven living in Chicago with a father who's a preacher, one of the first things I learned was how to speak up. It's because of these immutable truths that my public speaking experience began at a young age. I've been a poet, a stand-up comedian, a recruiter, a tour guide, a spokesperson, a professional public speaker - you name it, I've done it! Eventually and naturally, my love of speaking turned into writing.

Over the years, when friends and family got married, they started asking me to do the toast.

After a period of continuous requests, I became known as "the designated wedding speaker." In my curiosity to see if there was a need for wedding speech writers, I put up an ad online and soon discovered there was a huge market for it all over the world! I've written wedding speeches for people in Australia, Iceland, Indonesia, India - the list goes on and on! Here I was, in the unique position to help others by doing something that came completely natural to me. The rest is history. What I want you to understand is that YOU ARE NOT ALONE. I've written hundreds of speeches where people were nervous, inexperienced and downright terrified. When your emotions are going haywire, just remember this; a speech is just a conversation with many more people. How many debates have you had with friends over drinks? How many rounds of karaoke have you played knowing that your singing voice was terrible? You did it though, didn't you? That's my point! If you can do that then this is a piece of cake. Now I don't want you to think I'm downplaying a very real fear. I know just how real it is. The truth is that most people fear public speaking more than they do their own death! But why?

One of the main reasons is we just don't know what to say. Well, this book will solve that problem. But then, there are those who don't know how to say it and let me tell you, there are a million ways! You can deliver a speech as a song (which I've done and it was entertaining for the audience and fun for me), as a poem, in a specific theme, in a group, and more! But the key is to stay true to yourself. That's why at the beginning of this book I say the greatest part of the speech is YOU! The truth is that the Bride, Groom or both chose you because they like who you are and don't you forget that! As a matter of fact, I'll mention this again just to drive the point home. In the end what we're doing right now is just a game. No pressure … just fill in the blanks and I'll be right here to guide you!

HOW TO USE THIS BOOK

Ok, let's get down to business! This book is not the be-all end-all of wedding speeches. It's a starting point. Maybe you'll find a speech perfect for you in these pages or you might create a whole new speech inspired by the activities here. You'll notice that there are some blank pages with the word **'NOTES'** at the top. That's for the extra space you need or ideas you have. Just go for it! This book is for you so use it as you see fit.

It's broken down into three sections based on the desired emotional response you want from your audience, so there's no need to read it like a novel. Just jump to the section you think would fit your personality best.

1. **MAKE 'EM LAUGH** will help you write funny and sarcastic wedding speeches.

2. **MAKE 'EM CRY** will help you write heartfelt and meaningful wedding speeches.

3.   **MAKE 'EM SAY "AWWWW"** will help you write cute and charming wedding speeches.

The symbol key below will help to guide you through the writing process.

This symbol will give you suggestions of what to put in the blanks just in case you get stuck.

This symbol gives you an idea of who is best suited to give each speech.

And

This symbol explains how and to whom the speech would be best applied.

Also, in between each speech is a quote, phrase or statement that can be used as the starter, meat or even the toast or finale. Some of them have been revised a little. You'll see how I use them.

As a bonus, I threw in a freebie: a completed speech which gives you

20 speeches all together!

TIPS ON HOW TO HANDLE STAGE FRIGHT

1. Be Yourself! The truth is that the person who chose you to give this speech wanted you to be yourself, because they like who you are. So instead of getting up there and trying to be pretentious or someone you're not, tell yourself:

"It's okay to be myself."

2. Take a Deep Breath. Most people would be shocked to find out how calming it is to breathe deeply before speaking publicly. It's even one of the major relaxation suggestions in anger management. For more on breathing exercises you can use before giving your speech, check out this valuable website I found with tons of information on deep breathing exercises and benefits.

Go to **www.anxietycoach.com** and from the left side of the screen, click the "Belly Breathing" option.

3. Don't Rush! This happens all too often. If you speak too fast, everyone, including the bride and groom, will miss the awesome speech you put your heart and soul into. No one has to know it only took you 5 minutes or less to do it. So if you have trouble with slowing down, count to 5 in between each point to give yourself time to get through it. This also gives the audience a chance to really take in what you're saying.

4. Stay in One Place! Have you ever seen a child give a speech at church or school and noticed they were swaying back and forth like they had to go to the bathroom? Well, that might be cute for children, but for adults, it looks crazy! Keep your feet shoulder width apart so you have a comfortable stance and plant them to the ground. If you notice the audience moving but they're still sitting down, it's not them, it's you! Practice this one at home - believe me, it helps.

And last but certainly not least...

5. Have Fun! Even if you're giving a heartfelt speech, you have to admit that there is an element of excitement to being a part of such a great memory in someone's life. Have fun! And by that I mean feel everything you're saying. Allow your emotions to show and everyone will feel them with you … Okay! Let the games begin!

MAKE 'EM LAUGH

"*I wish you all the best in your life together.*"

~ Author Unknown

(Here's a practice exercise you can use to get your juices flowing.)

Best Friend/Best Man

This speech is great for a speaker who has a strong relationship with, spent a lot of time with or lived with the bride/groom.

(The bride and groom's names)

_____,

I told you that I'm terrible at speaking in public, so I hope you're not expecting some inspiring monologue worthy of receiving an Oscar for "Best Speech Performed at a Wedding."

When **(bride and groom's name)** _____met,

(Bride/Groom's name) _____ and I had a pretty awesome life!

We used to **(an activity you used to do together)**

_____.

We had a **(something you shared)**

_____ .

💡 *Something you shared could be: a true bachelor/bachelorette pad or a man cave filled with pleasures every man/woman could've ever dreamed of.*

We would laugh like we were kids. I had all this at my fingertips. But then, everything changed. **(groom's name)** _____ started spending more and more time with **(bride's name)** _____ and less and less time with me. I just have one question. Was it me?

No, but seriously, **(bride's name)** _____ , even though things changed when you came into the picture, you never made me feel left out. You never made me feel like I lost my best friend. You made me feel like I gained a new one. You're the best thing that ever happened to **(groom's name)** _____ . I've never met two individuals more **(adjective that describes them)** _____ ,

15

(adjective) _____ and **(adjective)**

_____ than you both are.

Here are some examples of adjectives that could be used for this speech; loving, kind, sweet, giving, etc.

A toast to the bride and groom! **(Toast)**

(I filled in the blanks for you, so you can see how it looks when it's done.)

Best Friend/Best Man

This speech is great for a speaker who has a strong relationship with, spent a lot of time with or lived with the bride/groom.

John and Sarah,

I told you that I'm terrible at speaking in public, so I hope you're not expecting some inspiring monologue worthy of receiving an Oscar for "Best Speech Performed at a Wedding."

When **John and Sarah**   met, John and I had a pretty awesome life!

We used to **hang out all night playing games and drinking.**

We had   **a true man cave filled with all the pleasures every man could've ever dreamed of.**

We would laugh like we were kids. I had all this at my fingertips.

But then, everything changed. **John** started spending more and more time with **Sarah** and less and less time with me. I just have one question. Was it me?

No but seriously, **Sarah,** even though things changed when you came into the picture, you never made me feel left out. You never made me feel like I lost my best friend. You made me feel like I gained a new one. You're the best thing that ever happened to **John.** I've never met two individuals more **loving, kind** and **giving** than you both are.

A toast to the bride and groom!

I wish you all the best in your life together!

"May laughter fill

your home and love

fill your hearts."

~Revised Irish Blessing

 **Best Man/Best Friend**

For a best man or best friend who wants to give humorous marriage advice using silly things you used to do together that made your friendship special

(Bride/Groom's Name) _____ it seems like it was just yesterday we were **(Fill in what you used to do or be)** _____. And here we are today at your wedding. I know it's overwhelming and there's no manual on how to stay happy and in love in your marriage, but here are some tips I think will help you both in married life:

Geeks, children, playing in the backyard, single, dreaming of finding the one, in a band (think of what you two used to do or be)

1. **(Groom's name)** _____, it's very important to make **(Bride's name)** _____ feel valued for what she does. So, whenever she

20

(Fill in something she does for you)

_____

Make sure you ask one question/make one statement to show

her your appreciation:

(An inside joke you share)

_____

Something she does for you*: cooks dinner, washes your*

clothes, cleans the house, runs and errand for you, etc.

Something you do to participate: *eating her dinner, wearing the*

clothes she washed, enjoying the clean house, benefited from the

errand she ran for you, etc.

Inside joke: *If you don't have one, create one that you'll say forever.*

(The secret: she'll always remember your wedding day whenever you

tell that joke, forcing her to feel warm and fuzzy)

2. There's no doubt that there will be times when boredom

kicks in and you'll need to fill it with something useful or fun. My suggestion? **(a silly activity you used to do together)**_____

Believe me. This will provide hours of laughter and entertainment.

Play hide and seek as adults, have special contests, arm wrestling, etc.

3. I'm sure that you'll have lots of get-togethers because you're such a likeable pair, so the only welcome gift that you should give your visitors is

(Something silly you used to make or give people as a practical joke)

_____

Your new friends will always put your parties on their "To Do" lists after that, guaranteed!

22

Arm pit song, burped song, wedgies, etc.

(Bride and Groom's name) _____, even

though ever since you first started dating your relationship has been

cutting into my **(a fun activity you do together less than before**

they were together)

_____ time with

my best friend,

I can honestly say that you've stuck it out all this time. So it only

makes sense, even in **(Bride/Groom's name)**

_____ and my world, that you would

choose each other to spend the rest of your lives together.

To the bride and groom!

"May laughter fill your home and love fill your hearts."

Cheers!

<u>NOTES</u>

"The difficulty with marriage is that we fall in love with a personality, but must live with a character."

~ Peter De Vries

Son/Daughter/Sibling/Best Man/Best Friend

For a bride/groom with a characteristic/ personality that stands out

(Bride/Groom's name) _____, as you've married my **(relation to you)** _____ - and I probably know him/her better than anyone else - I thought I should take this time to let you know what you've just gotten yourself into. You see, *"The difficulty with marriage is that we fall in love with a personality, but must live with a character."* With that thought in mind, I've compiled a list of rules entitled:

How to Stay Happily Married to a **("The Kind of Man/Woman They Are")**

_____

Metro sexual, obsessive compulsive, workaholic, shopaholic,

etc.

1. Don't be surprised if you walk into a room and see him/her **(something he/she might see that they only do in private)**

_____.

I only say this because there have been countless times when I've done the same, thinking **(Bride/Groom's name)**

_____ would be doing **(something normal)** _____ only to find him/her **(something bizarre they did that you've witnessed/something a person in that category would do)**

_____

_____

_____. I'm just saying, it's hard being a **(title)** _____, and sometimes you have to do certain things in order to be prepared.

2. A **(personality type)**

_____believes he/she **(something**

he/she blindly believes/does that he/she is horrible at)

_____

DON'T LET HIM/HER!

Brace yourself. This **(TV personality like him/her)**

_____ wanna-be is convinced that

he/she can **(an activity they think they can do but can't)**

_____

By the way: thanks, everybody for contributing to his/her

ridiculous worldview! Anyway, here are a few examples of things

you should not let him/her do...

- **(A hilarious example you witnessed that fits into #2)**

  _____

  _____

- **(Another hilarious example you witnessed that fits into**

  #2) _____

_____

True Story.

    3. Accept your **(title)** _____'s

    (something funny that he/she wears or goofy thing that

    he/she does that's a part of his/her character that they'll

    have to get used to because

    it isn't going away.)_____

    _____

    _____

Yes. I know he/she looks dashing right now in his/her suit/dress but

when this is over he/she'll be **(a funny example of him/her doing**

this)

_____

_____.

That's right. She/he takes his/her role seriously.

And finally,

4. Don't be jealous if your **(title)** _____

(something he/she gives a lot of attention to that may create this

emotion)

_____.

I know you can't believe it and he/she doesn't like most people to

know this but your **(title)** _____ has a **(adjective)**

_____side.

(An example of what he/she does)

_____

_____

It's true. There have been numerous times when I've walked into a

room only to find him/her doing just that.

But seriously, I'm so happy for both of you.

(Refer to Relationship) _____, I'm

honored to know a **(title)** _____ like

you. Thank you for your giving me the joy of being your best

man/best friend/being here/bride's maid/etc.

To the bride and groom!

I wish you all the happiness in the world as you embark on this new adventure.

Cheers!

<u>NOTES</u>

"The hunt is over!"

~Adam Levine

 **Best Man/Bride's Maid**

For a bride/groom who is an overachiever

(Groom's name) _____,

Being chosen to be the Best Man/Bride's Maid of the **(sarcastic overstatement of something he/she does well)**

_____ is an honor rarely

bestowed upon men/women like me. I know we regular" people can

be a bore but somehow you manage to live among us.

Fast language learner, mathematics genius, basketball aficionado, etc.

Just so that everyone knows … being the

(Sarcastic overstatement title) _____

has its perks.

Such as;

- **(An overstated super hero-esque example of something he/she's done in this title)**

_____

_____

- **(Another overstated super hero-esque example)**

_____

_____

- **(Another overstated super hero-esque example)**

_____

_____

Think of superhero abilities and compare it to what they do well. For example; faster than a speeding bullet, disappearing, super strength, etc.

And the list goes on and on.

Alas, everyone with super-human powers has their inner struggle. Superman had his status of orphan and alien as well as his kryptonite weakness; Batman had his relationship failures, and so on.

(Groom/Bride's name) _____ inner struggle was finding a wife/husband. And not just any wife/husband he/she needed a wife/husband that could **(characteristic that matches well for a man/woman of this type)**

_____ ,

Think of what type of characteristics work well together. If someone is a mover and a shaker, they may need someone who reminds them to slow down,

An introvert may need an extrovert and vice versa.

a wife/husband who was (**a characteristic of the bride /groom**)

_____, a wife/husband who would

both (**characteristic that balances**) _____

_____ and (**Characteristic that**

balances) _____, a

wife/husband that would remind him/her that he/she didn't have to

(**something the groom/wife might feel pressured to do to keep**

his/her status)

_____.

And finally, after many disappointing dates, *"the hunt is over."*

He/she found a match in (**bride/groom's name**) _____, who

is a powerhouse in his/her own right!

Their union signifies great possibilities, and to that I raise my glass to this couple in praise.

To the Bride and Groom!

May you stay consistent in your determination to love each other.

"I love being married. It's so great to find that one special person you want to annoy for the rest of your life."

~Rita Rudner

Sibling/Friend/Best Man

Sibling rivalry/ competitive siblings

(Nickname) _____,

I look at you today in your suit/wedding dress with your lovely/handsome bride/groom, and I can't believe you're the same person that **(something he did when you fought as kids).**

_____

_____

As kids, we challenged each other and laughed together. We shared things and **(a special memory of an activity you used to do together).**

_____

_____

There were times when we were angry at each other, and we'd make up shortly after.

Well, I don't know about you but I was mad at you at times.

40

You could never be mad at me ... I mean, I was perfect. I still am.

But in all seriousness, as many things as we've seen and done together, I'm glad that I got to experience this day with you. Your beautiful wife/wonderful husband **(a metaphor that describes how beautiful/handsome she/he looks)** _____

_____

I read a quote by Rita Rudner that said,

"I love being married. It's so great to find that one special person you want to annoy for the rest of your life."

So, in that spirit, if you ever need ideas on ways to really push his/her buttons, call me.

To the bride and groom!

May all of your differences make you stronger together, like they did for us!

NOTES

"A job is what we do

for money;

work is what we do

for love."

~ Mary Sarah Quinn

Groom,

Vows for bride/groom who loves his/her job, a bride/groom who's obsessed with his/her job or a bride/groom who is getting married to someone in the same field/industry/met on the job, etc.)

A Love Letter from a **(your job title)** _____, I've watched you from afar without knowing if you ever even noticed me. I see you in all the things that I do. As I **(something you do on your job)**, _____, I envision you **(doing something great involving your industry)**

_____. Your beauty/handsomeness is unmatched and your sweet demeanor calms me, reminding me of **(something that's really great to see in your industry)**

_____.

What can I say of my love for you? It will eternally last, like **(something beautiful in your industry)**

_____.

My anticipation grows stronger as we proclaim to the world our love for each other. Our love cannot be compared to **(something amateur in your industry)**

_____.

NO! That is puppy love. We have been destined since the beginning of time. Come to me and let me **(industry action/verb).**

_____.

I will be your **(job title)** _____
and yours alone.

(Bride/Groom's name) _____, you are my queen/king, my life partner, my lover, my support and my confidence.

Ultimately, _"A job is what we do for money; but work is what we do for love."_

And you make working easy.

NOTES

"Here's to a long life and a merry

one.

A quick death and an easy one.

A pretty girl and an honest one.

A cold beer and another one!"

~ Irish Blessing

Best Man, Bride's Maid, and Any Family Member who is a part of the culture the bride/groom is marrying into

This speech should be used when the bride or groom is going to be married into a culture they are not presently apart of.

(Bride and Groom's Name) _____ , I'm going to start this toast off by doing the only thing acceptable from a/ an **(the culture of the family the bride/groom is marrying into)** _____ family.

(Tell a funny story your culture and family is familiar with.)

_____

_____

_____

_____

As **(name of the person you're going to quote)**

_____ would say,

(Quote)

_____

_____

_____.

💡 *Make sure it's a cultural quote that has to do/matches with*

family.

(Bride/Groom's name)

_____, now I will welcome

you into our family with a tradition, (say or do something funny that

your family or culture customarily does to welcome people into the

family members)…

To the bride and groom!

(Quote a popular cultural blessing such as, for example if the family is Irish, the blessing below.)

"Here's to a long life and a merry one. A quick death and an easy one. A pretty girl and an honest one. A cold beer and another one!"

"Got your catch, now down the hatch!"
~ Adam Levine

&

"Vows are done, let's have some fun!"
~ Adam Levine

 **Best Man**

This is for a groom that you want to sarcastically accuse of being egotistical because he has more than one best man.

(Bride and Groom's Name) _____,

I just want to say that it's such an honor to be a part of a moment as great as this, in both of your lives. Really, I mean it. When you said I do I **(an overdramatic and sarcastic action)**

_____

An overdramatic and sarcastic action. It doesn't have to be true. The point is to be very sarcastic; for instance, cried, felt my heart skip a beat, etc.

OK. OK. So I'm laying it on pretty thick. I just did that to make

(groom's name) _____ feel better.

We all know how much he loves to get his ego stroked, hence the reason he had to have

(The number of best men) _____ best men to toast to the occasion.

Also, in an attempt to keep him happy, I plan on making a lot of random toasts!

So, here's the first one;

To the bride and groom!

Use any or all of the toasts below. Continue to make silly toasts throughout the reception. You'll realize that after a while, people will be expecting and even looking forward to it! They might even decide to do their own.

"You got your catch, now down the hatch!"

"Vows are done, let's have some fun!"

MAKE 'EM CRY

"May you find new reasons to love each other with each day that passes."

~Author Unknown

Sibling/Best Friend/Bride's Maid/Best Man/Parent

This is a heartfelt speech for bride/groom who you watched grow up/ grew up with

(Bride/ Groom's name) _____,

You're here. This is it. The day you've been waiting for since you were **(age)** _____ years old. I remember watching you **(an activity she/he and you both did to prepare for this day when he/she and you both were younger or a general activity; for instance, construct buildings with legos or decorate your doll house).**

_____. I could see then the care and **(an adjective for his/ her characteristic/ personality)** _____ you put into things. Your **(something about her that completes this statement for instance; energy, love, attitude, etc.)** _____ ignites a spark in everything you do and in everyone around you. You live, give and love effortlessly. No one is more deserving of fulfilling all their dreams and finding the perfect person to share their life with than you. I'm so proud of the woman/man you've become, and so blessed/lucky to be your **(relationship to the bride/groom)**

_____. Words can never express how beautiful/handsome you look today and the way your presence lights up the room. When I look at you both, I know you'll be happy together. I see the evidence in the way you treat each other, the way you respect each other and love each other.

(Bride/Groom's name) _____, it's a privilege to welcome you into our family/circle of friends and I'm glad to say that I have a new **(new relationship you are to the bride/groom, for instance, brother, sister, cousin, son in law, etc.)** _____ and that you have a new **(new relationship the spouse is to you; for instance, brother, sister, cousin, son in law, etc.)** _____.

💡 *Use the terms that represent your relationship to the bride/groom.*

A toast to the bride and groom!

"May you find new reasons to love each other with each day that passes."

I love you both.

Cheers!

"*My heart to you is given:*
Oh, do give yours to me;
We'll lock them up together,
and throw away the key."
~Frederick Saunders

 **Groom/ Bride**

Vows or speech from the bride/ groom describing how the person you are marrying makes you feel and what you'll promise to do and be for them

(Groom/ Bride's name) _____ ,

My love for you is endless but somehow continues to grow daily.

When you **(something he/ she does that makes you feel like the following)**

_____ ,

I'm comforted.

When you **(something he/ she does to you that makes you feel like the following)**

_____

me, I relax and feel free.

When you **(something he/ she does that makes you feel like the following)**

_____

me, I'm reminded that I wasn't always whole.

When you **(something he/ she did)**,

_____,

I fell in love with you all over again.

I know your heart is fragile, so I'll always handle it with care.

I promise to **(an action he/ she values)**

_____

and

(Another action he/ she values)

_____,

to make you feel like **(a way he/ she likes to feel)**

_____.

I promise to be your **(something he/ she needs)** _____

_____ and give you

and our family all the things we dreamed of as children.

I'll walk with you as your partner, careful not to run ahead or lag behind.

Our love life will remain as fresh and alive as it is today.

My vow is to be your friend and communicate with you,

working hard not to shut you out because you are the light of my life and without you, I'm in total darkness.

It's my job to hold our family in my arms and shield you from the world.

Take my hand, my darling, and never let go.

Be my King/ Queen for a lifetime,

And I'll be **(something romantic you want to be for him/ her for instance; "soul mate", or" Be my moon for a lifetime and I'll be your stars." Or "Be all mine today and I'll be yours forever.")**

_____.

"My heart to you is given: Oh, do give yours to me; we'll lock them

up together, and throw away the key."

 And I'll be your soul mate.

Or you could change the entire phrase: "Be my moon for a lifetime and I'll be your stars forever." Or "Promise/ Vow to be all mine today and I'll be yours forever."

NOTES

"Love does not consist of gazing at each other, but in looking together in the same direction."

~Antoine de Saint-Exupery

Parent/Grandparent/Older Family Friend

A speech that includes reflections and advice

(Bride and Groom's names)

_____,

Seeing you up there not only gives me great joy, but also reminds me of how old I really am. But age isn't bad. Marriage is a lot like wine. The older it gets, the better it tastes. I can say that's been true in my marriage and you will realize this too as the months roll into years. We, in this room, have watched you grow from children into well-rounded adults and now have witnessed you marry the love of your life. As you start this journey, in the words of **(person you're quoting)** _____,

(The quote)

_____.

(Explain the lesson learned from that quote)

_____.

And to take a quote from **(person you're quoting)**

_____,

(The quote)

_____.

(Explain the lesson learned from that quote)

_____

_____.

(Your wife/husband's name) _____ I wish

that as you begin your married life together, you remember that *"Love*

does not consist of gazing at each other, but in looking together in the

same direction."

Cheers!

NOTES

"Love is a symbol of eternity.

It wipes out all sense of time,

destroying all memory of a

beginning and all fear of an

end."

~ Madame de Stael

**Groom/Bride**

Vows that utilized the time you've been together to describe how you've grown into the couple you are today

For **(number of years together)** _____, you've been my friend.

For **(number of years together)** _____,
we've watched each other grow.

For **(number of years together)** _____, I've loved you unconditionally.

And **(for number of years together)** _____, you've done the same.

Today, we celebrate with our friends and family the beginning of our life together.

Today, I make it clear that **(number of years together)**

_____ is not enough.

"Love is a symbol of eternity. It wipes out all sense of time, destroying all memory of a beginning and all fear of an end."

Forever, I promise to be **(a. something you'll be for him/ her)**

_____.

Forever, I promise to **(b. something you'll do for him/ her)**

_____.

Forever, I'll get to **(c. something you'll get to see him/her do that you cherish)**

_____.

Forever, I'll get to **(d. something you'll get to hear him/her say that you cherish)**

_____.

a)   *Something you'll be: your lover or your partner*

b)   *Something you'll do: build a life that we can be proud of together, etc.*

c)   *Something you'll get to see him/her do: see you smile, etc.*

d)   *Something you'll get to hear him/her say that you cherish; need you (an inside joke could work here as well)*

And forever, I'll cherish every moment.

Before we met, I was **(what you were without him/her)**

_____.

Before we met, I **(something you used to do)**

_____.

When I first saw you, **(your reaction)**

_____.

The first time you looked at me**, (your reaction)**

_____.

The first time I asked you out/you asked me out, **(how you felt)**

_____.

The first time you held my hand, **(how you felt)**

_____.

The first time we kissed, **(how you felt)**

_____.

With my mind, I'll **(e. something you'll think)**

_____,

With my soul, I'll **(f. something you'll give him/her)**

_____.

e)   Something you'll think: always think of ways to show you how special you are, etc.

f)   Something you'll use your soul to be or do for him/her: give you more and more of me every day, etc.

With my heart, I'll love you forever

"There is only one happiness in life, to love and be loved."

~ George Sand

Mother/Father of Groom/Bride, Family Member of the Bride/Groom

I've always known you were special;

now **(bride/groom's name)** _____ knows it too.

I've always known you were **(something else you always thought about them)** _____;

now **(bride/groom's name)** _____ knows it too.

I've always pushed you to **(something you've encouraged them to be or do)**

_____;

now **(bride/groom's name)** _____ is pushing you too.

I've always believed you could **(something you always believe they could do)**

_____;

now **(bride/groom's name)** _____

believes in you too.

I've always been the one to **(something you've always done for them)**

_____;

now **(bride/groom's name)** _____will do that too.

I've always cherished your **(something you cherish about them)**

_____;

now **(bride/groom's name)** _____

cherishes that too.

I've always loved you unconditionally.

Now **(bride/groom's name)** _____ loves you just as much as I do.

Here's to *"love and being loved"* and to more and more of it!

Cheers!

NOTES

"The beginning of love is at the end of resistance."

~ Danielle Light

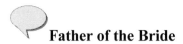 **Father of the Bride**

A speech for a father who is close to his daughter and was protective of her.

As your father, it was my job to

(a. 1 thing you felt it was your job to do)

_____,

One thing you felt it was your job to do: protect her, provide for her, make her feel special, etc.

(b. Another thing you felt it was your job to do)

_____ and to

(c. another thing you felt it was your job to do)

_____.

I saw you off on dates where I secretly threatened every guy that dared to mistreat you. Today, my job as your father has changed. I'm supposed to give you away, to turn you over to another man to be your **(repeat a.)** _____,

(repeat b.) _____ and to

(repeat c.) _____.

Though it's hard to let someone else fill those shoes, I find myself very happy at the same time because you've found a fine young man. I know in my heart that he'll do right by you.

So, even though you're a married woman, there's one thing that will never change: you'll always be my little girl.

A toast to the bride and groom!

May you remember daily *"The beginning of love is at the end of resistance."*

NOTES

"That was the moment I knew that I wanted to wake up next to you every morning."

~ Jerusalem Singleton

 **Bride/Groom**

Vows that use your memories together to reveal how you felt in the beginning and how you feel now

(Start with a memory that describes the line beneath the space.)

_____

_____

"That was the moment I knew that I wanted to wake up next to you every morning."

(Another memory that describes the line beneath the space)

_____

_____

That was the moment that I knew that I wanted to be the one to take care of you.

(Another memory that describes the line beneath the space)

_____

That was the moment that I realized I wanted to be with you forever.

You've blessed me by saying I do and I'll spend the rest of my life showing you how much I love you by being the only woman/the only man that you need and desire.

MAKE 'EM SAY "AWWW"

"They have the greatest pre-nuptial agreement in the world.

It's called love."

~Gene Perret

Parent/Grandparent/Friend/Bride's Maid

This speech utilizes puns and lessons learned

(Bride and Groom's names) _____,

I know this is the happiest day of your lives, and it should be celebrated as it marks a sign of love and commitment. But as I watched my **(relationship to you)** _____ run around making sure that EVERYTHING was perfect for his/her big day, **(a sarcastic pun about being a perfectionist)**

_____.

But I understand. You've been dreaming of this day your whole life.

Puns can be found all over the internet! An example of a pun: "It was a beautiful wedding. Even the cake was in tiers." Here are some websites that have some great ones you can use: www.punoftheday.com and www.wherethepunis.com

*You can also find some really cute puns on **www.pinterest.com**.*

I have a few things I want you both to remember because

1. **(Pun about making mistakes or not realizing how important or special something is)**

_____.

💡 *A pun that could work here: "Some people think marriage just has a nice ring to it."*

2. **(A lesson in marriage that they can learn from that pun)**

_____.

💡 *A lesson to be learned could be; don't let your marriage end up like this.*

3. **(Pun you think you can draw a lesson from)**

_____.

89

(A lesson in marriage that they can learn from that pun)

_____

4. **(Pun you think you can draw a message from)**

_____.

(A lesson in marriage that they can learn from that pun.)

_____.

And finally,

5. **(Pun you think you can draw a message from)**

_____.

(A lesson in marriage that they can learn from that pun)

_____.

I just want to say that the wedding was beautiful. **(A cutesy metaphorical pun to describe the wedding)**

_____.

"May you remember that you have the greatest prenuptial

agreement in the world: Love!" (Revised)

"To the beginning of

a beautiful forever."

~ Author Unknown

 **Best Man/Bride's Maid**

Speech that lightly embarrasses the bride/groom by pointing out unknown sweet things they did or said about their wife/husband

My job as **(position you are in the wedding party)**

_____ is to be a sounding board and all around support for the bride/groom. So, it's only fair that I get to embarrass them by pointing out all the cutesy stuff I noticed during the planning stage.

When we went to try on wedding/bride's maid dresses/tuxes, he/she

(Something cute and thoughtful they did/said)

_____.

When we were at the bachelor/bachelorette party he/she

(Something cute and thoughtful they did/said)

_____

And the morning of the wedding, he/she

(Something cute and thoughtful they did/said).

_____.

It's obvious he/she loves you very much, even in the smallest of actions and things he/she says. So here's *"to the beginning of a beautiful forever."*

Cheers!

NOTES

"True love stories

never have endings."

~ Richard Bach

Best Man/ Bride's Maid/Friend/Family Member

Life is filled with moments.

And I know you'll make them

(Something you'll believe they'll do with their time)

_____

because you're both

(Something in their characteristics that tells why they'll do this

with their time)

_____.

Life is filled with hopes.

I know you'll turn them into realities

because you're both

(Something in their characteristics that tells why they'll makes

their hopes come true)

_____.

Life is filled with fears.

But I know you'll get through them because you have each other.

Life is filled with magic.

And I know this because *"true love stories never have endings."*

Cheers!

"We've gained more riches than we could have ever asked for and that treasure started when you said,

"I do."

~ Jerusalem Singleton

Groom

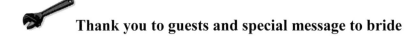 **Thank you to guests and special message to bride**

 **Freebie!**

I would just like to say to everyone how grateful we both are to have all of you in our lives. We know that you're here to celebrate our decision to spend our lives together, but this is not just a marriage between two individuals; this is a marriage between two families, two groups of friends and so much more! Mom and Dad, you're the greatest people and the most important examples in our lives. We couldn't have done this without you. And finally, to the woman I've chosen to spend the rest of my life with. The only woman I'll have eyes for until they close forever. Darling, you mean the world to me.

Thank you for choosing to share your life with me and for giving me so much more. And to top it all off, you also gave me more family and friends. When I look around this room I see how fortunate we are. Because of our decision, *"we've gained more riches than we could have ever asked for and that treasure started when you said, 'I do.'"*

Dear Reader,

First I want to say, congratulations to all the happy couples about to take that beautiful leap of faith purely based on love. I wish you all the blessings that your hands can hold. Thank you so much for buying this book.

If you made it to this page then hopefully you enjoyed the book and I would like to ask a favor. It's difficult for self published authors, like me, to compete with large publishing houses and have readers that would enjoy my book to find it. One of the best ways to do this is to have honest reviews of the book. The more reviews a book has, the more likely people are to purchase it when they come across the page. I would really appreciate an honest review of my book on Amazon.

Please join me at Facebook.com/JerusalemLSingleton and follow me on Twitter @jruism. I'd love to hear from you and what you thought about the book.

Until then …

Happy Writing and Speaking!

Best Regards,

Jerusalem Singleton

Made in United States
North Haven, CT
17 April 2023

35538378R00065